THIS IS THE FIFTH BOOK OF

TRANSMITTED BY

JONATHAN SWIFT

DEAN OF
ST PATRICKS CATHEDRAL
DUBLIN

with
amanuensis

IBSN. 978-1-84799-254-3

ALSO WRITTEN BY THIS AUTHOR

GET OUT

****

(For the sake of the children)

This is a dramatically good book about a woman's suffering during nineteen years in a marriage with an abusive man. She also tells you of the emotional damage it does to the children of such a liaison.

****

Also

POETRY BOOK. 1.

POETRY BOOK. 2.

POETRY BOOK. 3.
(with a twist)

POETRY BOOK. 4.
(assigned by J Swift)

All the poetic writings are delivered by a writer who died in the year 1745.

All published by LULU.com.

DEDICATION

****

This book and all the other books I have published are dedicated

Ever thanking him for all our privileges.

****

THE
PROLOGUE
****

I again feel, as Idid in my books one, two, three and four of published poems, that some things have to be explained. Just in case you have not read those previous publications here is what I said in those prologues.

I cannot take credit for these writings as I was only the instrument in their birth.
There are over a thousand such epistles which will be offered for publication in the future.
I personally got such healing from some of these poems, and I hope, by reading them, that pain relief reaches out to anybody in distress, as I was at the deaths of my two sons.

The inspiration for all these writings comes directly from the spirit of a gentleman who died in 1745, and he went by the name of Jonathan Swift.
Actually Jonathan Swift has been scripting writings through me since I was aged twelve. At that age I was very frightened, particularly as I had never even heard the name of this writer and did not really comprehend what was happening to me. Now over the years I have learned to accept it. I now get the greatest pleasure in the communion, and take great joy from the only lengthy and true friendship I have ever had.

I personally have had only a basic education and I always find myself rummaging in the ‘Chambers dictionary’, to find out exactly WHAT I have written down.

I find it hard to understand the way in which Swift expresses the words which have flown through my hand. Unlike me Dean Swift had a super education. There are a lot more epistles and anecdotes to accompany the future books I have planned.

I do hope you enjoy the writings and the accompanying, (some comic, some tragic) stories, but can I advise you, to read only one or two a day, to achieve the deeper understanding. Otherwise it may do to you as it did to me in the past, that is , to saturate your brain and comprehension.

May I offer you God's blessings dear reader and I sincerely hope that some of these writings speak to you and bring you comfort and healing as it is required.

Sincerely

Alexa Pope, **e.mail. alexapope@yahoo.es**
2008

INDEX

****

INDEX

****

(Continued)

1

ANNOTATION
(A message for all)

This is one of the most recent writings to come from Dean Swift.
He has in years gone by told of the earth's abuse, but, here I think he is sending out a stronger message to try to get through to everyone.
I understood the overall plea, but I must say some of the words I cannot find in my dictionary. Still I aim to go on as I have gone on for thirty five or more years, just writing these things down exactly as I get them, and changing nothing.

Yours sincerely Alexa.

A MESSAGE FOR ALL

****

Above the Babel hubbub, above the milling throng.
Above the grinning mien of dastardly ambition,
Are hoping, such holy hues, to fill your world with song.
Seraphic paragons expunge all dark derision.
A louder voice is heard amidst mindless confusion.
With knuckles blanched, our God will one day have his way.
The apt named dross, materialism, 'tis crass delusion'.
Denuded birth, naked death. This truth will always stay.
This missive says; strive please, to search your very centre.
Endeavour well, with time to think, to delve, to dig deeper.
Then when your meted time span benignly bids you, enter.
Still in bliss, serene of soul, greet the eternal reaper.
Entreating you, I beg of you, to heed my dire warning.
You enter death as you entered life, naked and alone.
Assistance will be there, to lead you to the morning.
I plead with all, I say again, atone, atone, atone.
Give total thanks to God above for privileges attained.
Then modest of mien, your guiding seraph will descend.
Stretch out your arms, with tears in flow and hands
unstained,
Finally to know, with joy aglow, this is not the end.

Swift.
August 5th 2008

Deo Gratis

ANNOTATION
(An old woman sighs)

How about this one?
This is exactly how I feel most of the time.
It just proves to me time and time again that my spirit guides know precisely what goes on in my earthly aura,
They give me a lot of strength to keep on refining my spirit. (Or at least trying to).
When the writing sessions are over,(sometimes only ten minutes or so), I get an immense release of tensions I have acquired during that particular day. So I hope these writings go on till my dying day.

Sincerely Alexa

4

AN OLD WOMAN SIGH'S
****

The heart lies dull, still beating in my breast.
My aching back moves slow to stand aloft.
My teeth, no longer bright, still howl for rest.
The digestion rumbles on, hard or soft.
I smile, I nod my head as well - as if I know.
My time, though limited is hanging long.
I see the trees, the sun,, sometimes the snow.
Longing am I , to sing to God, my song.
I lay me down, in prayer, in desperation.
I close my eyes,, but sleep eludes me still.
Nights are long – nocturnal exasperation.
My flesh complains and whines beneath my will.
I feel tis time to call me to my rest.
For what more is it , that I have yet to know?
In this allotment, I know I gave my best,
Four incarnations in one, I have to show.
This soul of mine is badly bruised and sore.
This ancient flesh I do not wish to take.
I've crammed much pain in this life, tis for sure.
A time for rest is what I now request.
A little time for silence I implore.
My life's light fades, asking, 'did I stand the test'?
Grant me my peace, for now and evermore.

SWIFT
10th August 2008

5

ANNOTATION
(Advice given)

This is one of the 1982 ones in which the powers that be were trying to give me a brighter day and a better life. They did manage to do that actually, as I, bit by bit became more spiritual in my outlook.
It was a learning time for me personally.
My spirit guides were delighted that I had at long last, started to notice them. They engineered many changes in my everyday life and instead of forever fighting a rising tide, I, all of a sudden, was swimming WITH the tide.
I could not lose.

Sincerely Alexa.

6

ADVICE GIVEN

****

You walked in morning's mists,
With clouded eyes.
Saw visions which you kissed,
The image dies.
Shackled now, with no relief,
Until you see.
Surrounding chains of disbelief,
Cannot break free.
Endowed with keener mind,
With keener thought.
Then loose the chains which bind,
Lest all for naught.
Think not to raise yourself,
To the higher waves.
Tis tantamount to self,
Against self raves.
For an unrestrained mind,
Should seek a way.
Now then, in seeking find,
A brighter day.

SWIFT.
(In the vibration of T.S.Elliot.)
25th March 1983

7

ANNOTATION
(A personal prophecy)

This is one where I am getting a small reprimand.
I think it was because I was not, at this time, sitting regularly enough. It took me years to trust and to not feel a bit of trepidation.
That came with time and we have such a close communion now that I can call on him at any time at all. He will always come.
This is the only male in my life that is worthy of my complete trust, and I give it completely.

Sincerely Alexa.

A PERSONAL PROPHECY

****

Hear me now,,, is it only I who sigh's?
As time goes by, do our fetid minds forget?
Tis only us, kept warm with brightened eyes.
Trying in our aim, to right the world e'en yet.
For time on time, the progress, slow but sure.
The elemental age is dead, can you not see?
Divinity eternally needs more.
May praying hands reach out, and set man free.
You grant we work as one,,, from my plane of life.
Materialists tell you nay, it matters not.
Stride forever forward, till we put paid to strife.
Sorrow, and pain,,, what hell has been your lot.
Now you have been endowed with your holy grail,
Our work, it shall be public, have no fear,
Be strong of spine, with heart, you will not fail,
Eternally, without a doubt, know I am here.
Many souls have been assigned this task together.
Thousands more, incarnate, will work as one.
With work and wit, and spirit in full feather.
We all may iterate, God's will, WILL be done.

SWIFT.
10th August 1972.

ANNOTATION
(A love missive)

This is me falling in love again!!!
Will I never learn? However at the time it felt like a good idea, and Dean Swift puts it all into words for me.
If you notice he does not give me any advice he just lets me go my own sweet way. You see, he cannot encroach on my God given free will. I have to be allowed to make my own mistakes, and in doing so I am supposed to learn.
Sometimes I do!!!!
What do you think?

Sincerely Alexa.

A LOVE MISSIVE

****

Come talk to me of wondrous ways and days.
Come walk with me with kisses flowing free.
Come list a while, hear songs my heart still plays.
Come love me now, my love bursts forth from me.
Come hear with me the music of the sure.
Come feel with me this unison of ours.
Come breathe with me a lover's air so pure.
Come gaze into my eyes, and fill the hours.
Come take my hand and know we are as one.
Come nestle close, your head upon my breast.
Come closer now,- and when this life be done.
Come lie with me,- transfixed in total rest.

SWIFT
20th February 1982

11

ANNOTATION
(Be still my heart)

What about this one?
I do invite my readers to formulate an opinion on these writings.
Does it ring a bell with you?
It of course does with me . Swift seems to be 'plighting his troth' again and trying to continually reassure me, do you agree?
My e.mail is alexapope@yahoo.es.
If any writing in these books means something to you, please let me know.
I really think that these epistles are not only sent for me, but must resound to a larger audience.
Sincerely Alexa.

12

BE STILL MY HEART
****

**Be still my heart, your thoughts with mine transcending,
In higher arc, soaring on strands of love.
We humbly ask, through purple mists descending,
With whitest thoughts, as plumage on a dove.
In spirit now we both progress together,
You in your small corner, and me, watchful, in mine.
This trust between us not even God will sever,
This wondrous work we do is of his plan, divine.
So as you bend your head and bid me enter.
As you open up your heart and still your soul.
With one accord, I am decreed your mentor,
To cast light upon the shadows is our goal.
As we sit as one and send our thoughts to heaven,
Twill be carried far to the utmost golden sphere.
If time, corpus and thoughts are freely given.
My word is yours, impregnable, - always here.
We shall excel, as always, we shall succeed.
Be not afraid, aegis, an aeon knows no bounds.
Your vital wants supplied, - more than you need.
Ubiquitous, safeguarding, I will stand my ground.**

**Swift.
(no date on the original)**

ANNOTATION
(My love)

I have decided to include this love writing because at the time this man was the greatest love of my life. I had never been in such raptures before. I was about thirty- nine at the time, and I believe if you fall in love aged one hundred it is still the same. I completely fell, hook line and sinker, and I still bear this gentleman's name. He is now in the after life, and waiting patiently for me.
That to me is very comforting.

Sincerely, Alexa.

14

MY LOVE

****

Come clasp my hand, I'll merge you with my soul.
Come soothe my brow, my lips are pursed to kiss.
You are my heart, my core, my only goal.
Come hold my hand and all this world dismiss.
I feel your breath, so warm, I smell you close.
I sink into a divine pleasure,,, rare.
The greatest love in all this world, - I chose.
With the whole world, this passion I will share.
For me, since time began, I can't perceive,
A greater love than this, since earth began.
Devotion I have offered, devotion I receive,
I breathe this balm, as I live out my span.
I deeply feel, this man and I, have been,
Entwined through other lives, by laws of God.
And whether he be beggar and I be queen,
The ordained meeting crossed the paths we trod.
I yield my soul, my breath, in expectation.
Complete immersion, I needing no other.
My eyes expand in staring adoration.
I need to feel nor see no other lover.

SWIFT
10th June 1981.

ANNOTATION
(Be inspired)

Here he was again,(Dean Swift) uplifting me when I was suffering a very bad depression. I lost two of my sons in tragic circumstances and I thought that I too would die. It was only the ministrations of my spirit guide that kept me from committing suicide at that time.
I had panic attacks, sleepless nights, actually it was the whole nine yards.
I leaned on him very heavily and it helped very much. I sometimes worry about all those people who have no faith, whatever do they do when hit with a big problem like that? However if this writing you can align to, please take it as yours.

Sincerely Alexa.

16

BE INSPIRED

****

Panicked am I, when all around is still.
Dismayed I feel, when viewed with sightless eyes.
I wildly thirst when all have drunk their fill.
Frantic I am when deaf ears hear no cries.
Annoyed am I, when on my righteous way,
Frenzied I feel when feeling is in vain.
Scared I am, as I lunge from day to day.
Deranged I am when I feel only pain.
Try to be awed, to glimpse the beauteous sky.
Now, lifted be to see the new born morn.
Now be elated, as velvet nights go by.
With bated breath, to greet the new pure dawn.
So be happy, to hold within your palm,
A tender leaf - axed from a tender tree.
Then hold a rose which ne'er conceives no harm,
In veined translucent beauty, lifted be.
Accept, that of this world - all is for naught.
Exception.
Evil is not your bent during your span.
Baleful response - either by deed or thought,
Tis not admitted into the master plan.
So panic not and look for a new way,
Contented be and look towards your goal.
Be honourable, get on your knees and pray.
Give thanks to God for being, feeling whole.

SWIFT
19th June 1983

ANNOTATION
(Unnecessary ire)

This was again a very gentle admonishment to me, as in my youth I was prone to get very het up in cases of injustices I came across from time to time.
He was right of course, because I came to realize that by getting angry I could NOT change anything. All I was achieving was my loss of energy, and I learned to channel it another way. I am sure some of you can align with the sentiments of, 'Unnecessary ire'.

Sincerely Alexa.

UNNECESSARY IRE
****

**When calm aggression boils,
In desperate phase.
When burdened down with toils,
In greyish haze.
When blackest humour burns,
With white hot blaze.
The offered kindness spurns,
In heated craze.
When fear subsides and ire dies,
In thinking's maze.
With gentle heart and gentler sighs,
Sweet music plays.
Then look around with misty eyes,
For happier days.
Do not allow these deadened souls,
Their evil praise.
Enter not their dirty holes,
To learn their ways.
Be punctilious, aloof,
We know the devil pays.
Know, my rede is all in truth,
Dispatch this malaise.
Do not be burned by hellish ire,
Be waving it away,
Wax in light, and wane in fire,
Then know a calmer day.**

**SWIFT
(In the vibration of T.S.Eliot).
10th April 1979.**

ANNOTATION
(Silent subtleties)

This writing conveys to me that I have done the right thing in allowing these writings to be published. Dean Swift wrote years ago, that this work would be published,,, but of course I thought it was bunkum,,, but now after all is said and done , whatever he says ,ALWAYS comes to pass.
He also is telling me that he is content with the communion, of which I am very happy about. Sometimes I strive to include these very personal writings, which are mine alone, but, I think it adds to the whole tapestry, don't you?.

Sincerely Alexa

20

SILENT SUBTLETIES

****

Well, now in deepest silence feel my love.
I hold your hand in mine and give support.
We walk composed, with contracts made above.
We toil, we help, we give with no retort.
The trials are near over, but, keep your faith.
Allow no man to gainsay our rarest work.
That stout heart within you, not one can shake.
And still, with all your pain, you hold no hurt.
A million years in your plane count for naught.
Unless the human soul is gently whitened.
For black is black, by word, or deed, or thought.
But good thoughts live, with this, your life is brightened
If you still do, as our oaths paired long ago.
I will remain, in silent shades, in robes of white.
With subtleties, we walk the road we know.
Rejoicing I – we walk towards the light.

SWIFT.
09.08.2008.

ANNOTATION
(Happy am I)

How about this one?
I think Dean Swift was saying we are managing to do the work we have been assigned.
After a long time of him trying to get me going, I think he is throwing me a rose.
Do you think YOUR spirit guide might be trying to align with you.
Let me know, I thank God every day for this gift, that I had the courage to allow this lovely spirit into my life. Do you think you can unlock your mind?.
If I can help you to communicate with your main guide e.mail me, and I will certainly give it a try. e.mail: alexapope@yahoo.es.

Sincerely Alexa.

HAPPY AM I

****

Happy am I when love encompasses my heart.
Happy am I when clear eyed, new horizons scan.
Happy when feeling, my love and me ne'er part.
With loves communion close, happy am I.
At dawns awakening I see my lover's face.
Deep in the night I feel his pulse, his heart beat.
Has there ever been through out this human race?
Two souls which roamed ten thousand miles to meet?
To meet by chance, and know,, within one instant,
Oh God, he is for me, and I for him returned.
This beauteous love, for me forever distant,
This emotion ever given, never spurned.
It's as gentle as a fragile spider's web.
As powerful as a mighty earthquake's roar.
My lost soul re-lives with every flow and ebb.
Now consuming me, till I can love no more.
With every gesture, and every silent move,
My love, to me, seems ever closer still.
Happy am I to have known and felt such love.
I entreat it lasts forever, with God's will.

SWIFT.
26th October 1981.

ANNOTATION
(Criticism)

This is a criticism of the way we are treating our planet.   This was written in 1981,,,, a long time before it was fashionable to be 'Green'. Now this was information given to me that I should have acted on at that time, but I didn't, so in this case I failed in my duty.
I was afraid that I would be ridiculed and my small children would be upset, but now Twenty five years later, I don't give a toss. I am putting these out now for the consumption of the public and the powers that be and if they don't agree with the sentiments in all of my five poetry books, I could care less. I hope you, my reader, like it, I certainly do.

Sincerely Alexa.

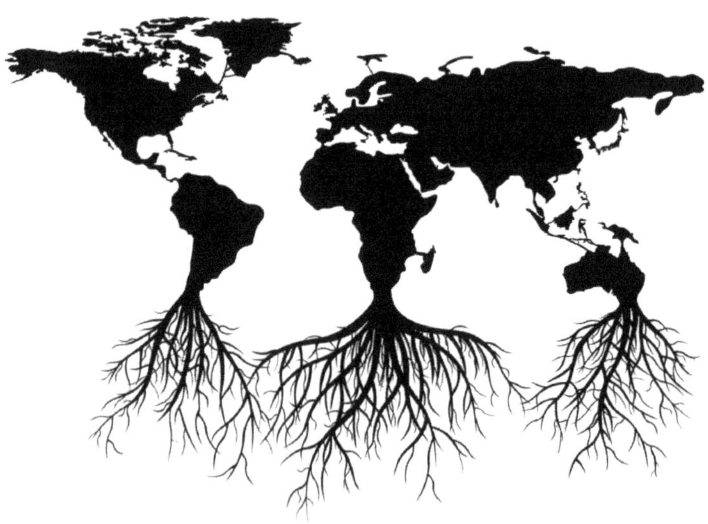

CRITICISM

****

Can the minds of men, still, ceaseless slumber?
Stay perpetually blind, these countless eyes?
Retarded are men's wits, and without number,
Awake I cry, before your earth's demise.
When will the minds of men eventually grasp?
This beauteous orb hurls steadfast to her doom.
It matters much as viewed in eons past.
If none will wake, all will be gone too soon.
A way now must be forged to shake these sleepers.
To stir the very breast of those who will,
Turn men from hate to love, devoid of weepers,
Then breathe a sigh and work unceasing still.
Tis only, born of nymph, can halt this rot.
Twill be a hard climb back, tis often said.
Now hear this plea, this earth is all you've got.
Sustain this raze, your world is now,, as dead.
The hellish wars, the angry deaths, the greed.
The zoic interbreeding, contra - cosmic law.
The Guillotine is poised, and will proceed,
To cleanse the earth of man. You ask, 'What for'?
For man is turning creation into paste.
Is edaciously chewing defecation.
So before all is toxic and laid to waste,
Comply with our ethereal expectation.
You are gifted, free will, but will you use it?
Tis actually a palpable product fault.
To use, free will for greed, seems you abuse it.!!
En masse, come down to earth with one vast jolt.

Swift. October 6th 1981.

25

ANNOTATION
(Philosophical thoughts)

What do you think about this one? I know this has been touted since the world began, (to love one another), but as far as I am concerned if Dean Swift says it, it must be true!!!
I know it is very difficult to love and forgive someone who has hurt you,,, but you MUST do it ,,,,for the transfiguration of YOUR spirit. You are the only one responsible for that. That is the reason you are here in this incarnation and in the set of circumstances you find yourself in. It teaches you lessons and these lessons have to be taken on board. I have proved this to myself, so you do your own bit of proving and then see.

Sincerely Alexa

26

PHILOSOPHICAL THOUGHTS

****

The sands of time it seems will cease to flow.
The murky tides of mans inhumanities
Will cease to ebb – and then in knowing, know,
How deathly fragile are man's fraught frailties
For strength is found, not in the worlds aggressors,
Tis laid within the simple hearts of them,
Who gently stand and view the world's assessors,
Who understand the violent moods of men.
You ask, 'What can we do,' - a dire task.
The only way is love, - teach love to all.
Then grow in love, - expand in love, we ask.
Then one by one the hating minds will fall.
For deep within each soul there lies a need.
To love and lov'ed be is each ones right.
For love can conquer jealousy and greed.
Brotherly love in its own right can fight.
But serenely is the loving battle fought,
In every passing mood, in every greeting.
In every deed and smile, in every thought.
In long lost friends, in every perchance meeting.
So pour out love once more in greater measure.
Live – love and learn by this philosophy.
Abounding back to you- ten fold, this treasure,
That your own mind and soul will rais'ed be.

SWIFT
7th September 1981

ANNOTATION
(Suicidal thoughts)

Here we are again, with Dean Swift speaking to me directly. I have included it s I know that many people have these thoughts at some time. I actually suffered for six years with post natal depression, before anyone had ever heard of it. I had no help and tried to commit suicide twice with two hospital admissions.

It was only when I had my middle son that I know the difference between the depressions. The moment he was born it was as if the world had been lifted off my shoulders and for the first time in six years I found I could lift my head up. Still its all for the learning, isn't it. I'm still here to tell the tale. But thank God now-a-days young women can get some medication for it and be helped. This writing might help someone out there to keep smiling. That is my hope anyway.

Sincerely Alexa

SUICIDAL THOUGHTS

****

The mind is numb, in fevered torment binds.
In sinking sands, in mires of self distrust.
You wring your hands, your severed soul still finds.
To death's own door your very will is pushed.
You wallow helpless as a babe in arms.
The piteous cries are for yourself alone.
You need a goal, a goal which soothes and balms.
A vista glimpsed which cries repent, atone.
Then glorious day, when chains of fear break free.
Refreshed and happy, whole, and filled with soul.
You'll thank God for the life he's given thee.
Then live again and strive to reach your goal.
Do not allow this world to bend and ride you.
These deathly thoughts you know that you can tame.
If you decide to douse the flame inside you,
You will return again, again, again.

SWIFT
1st May 1981.

ANNOTATION
(Night shades)

Here is another one pertaining to the night. There have been many times in my times of bereavement, and in times where sleep was impossible, I have sat at my bedroom window for hours and just waited for the dawn to rise. I am sure many of you have experienced that devastation, so maybe this writing touches you personally and you get the sentiments right away.

Sincerely Alexa.

NIGHTSHADES

****

The absence of the moon leaves night shades dying.
The spluttering stars can no longer stay the gloom.
The night hues creep,- well mourned, lost and sighing.
Denouncing deeper doubts to their dying doom.
The shroud of night encircles all who view it.
This validated void – what terrors must it hold?
With grasping claws – with prayers to see us through it
With visions rare – what nightmares can be told.
Then moonlight shafts appear – my God what splendour.
A silver strand to cast a silver glow.
Begone foul dark – enlist me dreams so tender.
This silent Queen who sees all I want to know.
Her riding high, this whole world is glittering.
Her enigmatic smile, her territory intact.
No foot of man, no devils, no birds twittering.
Observing all,, none to betray. Her role, exact.

SWIFT
30th July 1981

ANNOTATION
(Sealed with a kiss)

Here we are. This is me, just out of eighteen years of a domestically violent situation. I had to leave the country to get away from the animal I was married to,(see; 'GET OUT' (for the sake of the children). This book was written by me, warts and all.)
I went to live in Spain and start my life again in peace. It was here I met one of the greatest loves of my life, and obviously this union was sanctioned by Dean Swift by the receipt of this epistle. Maybe someone out there can completely align with the sentiments expressed here, if so please e.mail me at, alexapope@yahoo.es

Sincerely Alexa.

SEALED WITH A KISS

****

How now in deepest essence, feel the chord.
How deeper now, are your two lives entwined.
With utter love, you, frightening waters ford.
With adoring power, with loving hopes enshrined.
You walk as one - your pathways looking brighter.
This love you know will fill your very soul.
With every step, emotions lifting, lighter.
This tender swain, will make your being whole.
Twas late perhaps - but now your spirits blend.
With lessons learned - yet learning still goes on,
Remember this you will, till your life's end.
Aye, the stream of eternal love flows on.
When questions vex, and hearts around are sore.
When half of you still yearns, to live and love.
The best was done - a score of years,- no more.
What can more wasted time to each one prove.
So live and love and work and stand in grace.
Once wasted time is done - it ne'er returns.
Advance you shall, then breathe, then find your pace.
The love you found is that which spirit yearned.
For forty years you searched, then found at length,
This soul, with whom prior countless roads you trod.
This union now filled with compassionate strength.
Take it as given - a precious gift from God.

SWIFT
22nd November 1980

ANNOTATION
(One more step)

From the words in this writing I take it that I would take some flak from people who do not have this knowledge.
A few years ago I would have been worried about that, but now I could not give a damn.
Now ! What about the word 'Crapulent'.
I misconstrued the meaning of it until I looked in the, 'Collins dictionary'. You can imagine what I thought it meant!
It actually means, a drunkard.
It was the one and only time I have thought to change the word that came through. I did'nt of course. But I had to check on it before I included it in the final draft of this writing.

Sincerely Alexa.

ONE MORE STEP

****

The time will come when we shall, no doubt, stand,
Ill judged by idiot savants.
Our name may spread throughout this craven land,
Dashed low by adroit tramps.
Plough straight the furrow, - your head held high,
Show them no obvious pain.
We both, will not allow our link to die,
Tis strong and well, this chain.
Take pains to keep the tiller pointed straight,
There are new roads to travel.
Now strengthened be, in truth, you know your fate,
All mysteries unravel.
Let crapulent men still rant, still rear, and rave.
Let the godless scream their fill.
Permit them to die, with the drugs they crave,
We stand, well girded, still.
Lift up your face, we like to see you smile,
With consummate fervour.
Let dullards, dopes, dissenters, taste their bile,
Undaunted, we step further.

SWIFT
29th July 1990.
This writing is a mixture of Swift and Eliot's vibes.

ANNOTATION
(Another prophetic missive)

Here is another prophetic one ,as the name implies.
I thought long and hard as to whether or not I should include it as it is quite a personal message to me. Well, I thought you may like to know that sometimes I get a rose thrown at me for my diligence, and in this epistle it happens to be a golden one.
I take that as I am doing OK with the job I have taken on,,,,sooooo,,,, that will do for me,,,, I hope you agree.

Sincerely Alexa.

ANOTHER PROPHETIC MISSIVE

****

How now in sweet surrender, feel the chord.
With harmonies divine of purest essence.
Of loving thoughts, of heartfelt sighs out poured.
Of mercy missions, rebounding love, in blessings.
I offer you my heart, my soul's vibration.
To have, to hold, to use for your upliftment.
To feel me near, with alerting sensations.
An oh, so subtle signal gently different.
As progress comes more power can be tethered,
We work as one, our copular slow but sure.
Our destiny entwined, souls never severed.
Our task shall be accomplished perhaps more.
In the space of your earth time year by year.
Shall hunger to listen to what I shall impart.
Shall travel far,- from you own lips, they hear,
Devotion's of our souls, secret's of God's heart.
I send you a golden rose in spirit form.
I know you cannot forget your sacred word.
Your promised protection will never be shorn.
Give thanks, one day we will be fully heard.

SWIFT
(Circa 1990.)

37

ANNOTATION
(The graduation of,)
LEE

This is a writing that came through the day after my remaining son graduated from university. This was the way he tried to deal with the death's of his two brothers, he completely immersed himself in his studies. He was actually in university for about seven years and came out with three full degrees in medicine and physics and all with honours. He is now an airline pilot in America.
Well done to him. I was delighted.

Sincerely Alexa.

THE GRADUATION OF
****

****

Your darkened clouds have soared and changed to dust.
To what effect?
Your nemesis has starred - and with what thrust?
Crass intellect!!
You stand in robed array - with sprig in hand,
What to perfect?
Dismissed by you - the mires of sinking sand.
Your head erect.
You need your solid wisdom, your naked views.
To, what detect?
Your pointed questions asked, your mind ensues,
What to expect?
To give your love, to give your life, your whole,
To re-direct,
Your destiny, yearning to reach your goal,
With just respect.
Your internal wrath is o'er, that dirty fight,
To resurrect
The cosmic law, the way, the truth, the light.
So just accept.

SWIFT.
(In the vibration of T.S.Eliot.)
No date on the original.

ANNOTATION
(A man from hell)

This little poem was penned when Jonathan Swift conveyed to me that I should try to forgive my second husband. This is the man that the first book I wrote, 'GET OUT, (for the sake of the children)', was about.
I was eighteen years in a hellish partnership with this animal, and his behaviour completely emotionally disabled my children, resulting in my youngest aged 22 and my oldest aged 32 both committing suicide. I wrote this book, 'warts and all'. It was a God sent catharsis for me. Still when I was asked to give forgiveness, at that time I could not. I still have not, but I know I will have to look at it again, because NOT forgiving really damages the one who will not forgive. I still bear that cross.

Sincerely Alexa.

A MAN FROM HELL

****

When penetrating deep, this wound of hate,
Just terrified.
When thrusting on, mans violence to sate,
Just petrified.
The reconciliation no more can be,
Just mortified.
With senseless eyes, his violence still can see.
Just vilified.
Scarlet anger must one day cease to lust,
Be mollified.
And violence die, in one eternal thrust.
To pacify.
To exonerate this cur, how can you ask?
I'd rather die.
Let him fry in hell's halls, tis his failed task.
To justify.

SWIFT
(in the vibration of T.S.Elliot.
4th June 1983.

ANNOTATION
(An accolade)

This one is a reassurance once again to me. I think he is always aware of the chance of someone in the flesh will deride me or embarrass me, but my faith in him is stronger now than ever.
Everything he has promised me has come to pass. He even went and looked for my youngest son,(aged 22) when he passed away, and he brought him to me, and even though my son could not directly speak to me, (in accordance to cosmic law) he spoke to Swift and Swift relayed it to me. (See book 1 page 32). Uncanny isn't it. Still I hope you like the writing.

Sincerely Alexa.

AN ACCOLADE

****

We still can link as through the realms I travel.
We willing are, to stand by full of aid.
Life's lessons are the chords we will unravel.
The promise to you kept, the vow was made.
We work together, - non shall come between us
Calm will ensue, so lift the pen to write.
Serene you are, we look on well. It ne'er does
To stumble in the mire,,,, when all is light.
We show the path, we send you help, we love you.
We tell you time again,,, please listen well.
There's earth beneath your feet, the sky's above you.
We work as one,   as all your fears I quell.
Tis all in light, the future sleeps before you.
Tread firmly now – all promised will be given.
The months of rest were sent to well restore you.
Your head stands high, your morning sun has risen.

SWIFT
11. November 1981
(In the vibe of T.S.Eliot)

DEO GRATIS.

ANNOTATION
(Love and Live)

This advice came through soon after I managed to extricate myself from the horrendous eighteen year long marriage I was in. (See book 'GET OUT' (for the sake of the children). Published by Lulu.com.
I obviously did not want to even SEE another man, not even on my periphery. This writing was given to me on the first night I met my next husband. I did become his bride! He was one of the greatest loves of my life, and I am glad I took Swifts advice.

Sincerely Alexa.

LOVE AND LIVE
****

The man stands by your side.
So love and live.
On crests of waves you ride.
To love and live.
Suffus'ed souls will bide.
So love and live.
Tis not a sin to hide.
Give love to live.
Forget the days you cried.
Just love and live.
Let sunny days abide.
Please love and live.
With arms outstretched he tried.
His love to give.
Accept to be his bride.
THEN LOVE AND LIVE.

SWIFT
(in the vibe of T.S.Elliot)
11. November. 1990.

ANNOTATION
(Bertrand Russell)

What do you think about this conundrum.
This spirit, Bertrand Russell only came into the frame this one and only time!
I wrestled with the decision to include it, but here it is.
Don't ask me about the foreign names that are included it must mean something to somebody, but it isn't me. If it's you, do e.mail me. alexapope@yahoo.es.

Sincerely Alexa.

BERTRAND RUSSELL

****

Come sit with us recount and talk,
In philosophical galleries rare.
With Kant and Nietzsche, Swedenborg,
Confucius and Cardinaire.
We mull around the skepsis mire.
Of man's forage and looming,
Acceptance of mans dread, eternal fire,
Of neutron waves consuming.
The spirit Kant says – give to man,
The rope by which he dangles.
The Nietzsche soul says, 'If man can
Release the grip which strangles.
For these philosophising souls.
Each has their own base theory.
And each will strike their muted goals.
From which lesser minds would weary.
For Swedenborg, whilst in the flesh,
Perchance he found the key.
Our world was now to start afresh.
Tis theory versus philosophy.

SWIFT.
In the vibration of Bertrand Russell.
13th September 1982

ANNOTATION
(Do not judge)

What do you think of this one? He is telling us all not to set ourselves up as judge and jury of other mortals. It is not one of my favourite writings,,, but,,, I still think it was worth including. It may say something to a lot of you, just to keep in mind, 'Do not judge other people'.
Ahh well,,,,,,,,,,,,,,.

Sincerely Alexa.

OOP'S.

DO NOT JUDGE

****

Fie, show these mortals exactitude of rules.
Show just how puny physical man can be.
Awake these puerile materialistic fools.
Eternal portals swing, then look and see.
Who ordained you judge and jury, tell me who?
Who gave you precedence, I'd like to know?
In all this universe, an insensate few,
Inflate their egos and let their juices flow.
To set themselves above, what tomfoolery's.
Vainglory is a raiment. Tis best worn black.
Who in God's name gave these abject sublunary's
Their perfection, and so, the power to attack?
As God is my judge, acme will not be yours.
Damm not others, lest you too be dammed.
Corrupt incarnates, displaying all these flaws.
These selfish innuendos were never planned.
Review your life. Are you this man. Then pause.
For judging others is not your primary task.
If ignorant of the law of effect and cause.
For your own sake, on your own knees, just ask.

SWIFT.
(8th May 1982)

God is the only judge.

ANNOTATION
(Heartfelt)

This one is evidence that Swift is in my mind from time to time. He is not there all the time but he usually has to clear MY thoughts before he can commune clearly.
I do, as do you, live in this very thick worldly vibration and suffer the same consequences and pain as anyone else, and I repeatedly thank my God for Swifts ministrations.

Sincerely Alexa.

HEARTFELT
****

I wrung my hands – a touch – I held my breath.
A needed sigh.
My ache will carry me thro doors of death.
I plead, I cry.
With heart like lead, my eyes will watch the dawn.
I ask, Oh! Why?
Why give me love, then wish I was not born?
Beseeching I.
What wrong do I, as to be left for dead?
I will not lie.
I hold certain standards, well fixed in my head.
Pie in the sky?
Why do adulterous misfits latch on to me?
They are not shy.
Is it too much to ask, “ love faithfully”?
I want to die.
My nucleus, is stitched and patched again.
Do not deny?
Does each one fall in love, then feel such pain?
Or solely I?

SWIFT.
(In the vibe of T.S.Eliot)
3rd July 1981.

ANNOTATION
(Given for all who will listen)

I found this writing screwed up at the bottom of the box. It had only been half finished, so I decided on the 25th of September 2008 to finish it off and include it in this book number 5.

I don't think it was sent for me only. As the title says it was transmitted to try and teach anybody who needed to be taught. So if it only opens the soul of one person reading it, it and I have done my job. If it speaks to you please e. mail me.
alexapope@yahoo.es

Sincerely Alexa.

GIVEN FOR ALL WHO WILL LISTEN

****

We earnestly endeavour to try to teach,
The absolute truths so everyone must know.
What dizzy heights each soul can grasp and reach.
When your flesh is no more, where do you go?
Well list awhile the story shall begin.
Striving to educate your line of thought,
when flesh is dead and past, you enter in,
whatever plane your actions there have wrought.
Guides will wait and take the time for you to grow.
Waiting for you to realise what you must do.
For time is as naught, Eternity is slow.
Each step along the way, they'll bolster you.
You are answerable for all your actions.
In thought, in word, in deed and things undone.
These particles of life, these countless factions,
will fuse, softly sighing, thy will be done.
If it should be, you do not heed my words,
or waste the time allotted in this carnose.
You will once more pass with all the herds
Of sinful souls waiting to decompose.
So gravely we plead, keep to the narrow path.
You know in your own depths what you must do.`
Do not incur your Holy Father's wrath.
With arms outstretched, we put our faith in you.

SWIFT.
Half of this done with no date showing on original.
The second half done 25th September 2008.

ANNOTATION
(Do not deny our God)

This little epistle was another one that was only half finished. So I finished it.
I like it actually. It is for all those who say there is no God. I also agree that when they are breathing their last breath they will be flippin' well hoping that I'm right.
If it speaks to you, please let me know. This writing is certainly not for me, because I have never denied that there is a God. I am very happy to live with the fact that there IS.

Sincerely Alexa.

DO NOT DENY OUR GOD

****

In searching forms of life – why should man be
Staunchly arrogant.
A myriad heaving lives in your own body, see
Deadly decadent .
Look to these other worlds, symbiotic, all
Exuding pores.
All forms of life live in you. Fie! Stand or fall
By effect or cause.
To them YOU are the God, that some deny.
What base hypocrites.
Do not deny our God, as they, is my reply.
What muted lunatics!
I will preach here, twill stand you in good stead.
With your last sight.
Whilst gasping your last gulp, then chilled, then dead
You ‘ll hope I’m right.

SWIFT
(In the vibe of Eliot)
First half transferred 27th July 1980
Second half transferred 28th September 2008.

ANNOTATION
(Let us help)

This one is one of the older ones when they were trying their best not to lose the connection. I must have put them through hard times. Thank God I got rid of my fears and decided to complete the oath I had given before my reincarnation. From that moment I have never wanted for anything in this material world and everything they have purveyed has come to pass. Especially Dean Swift has never faltered from his continual protection and love for me.
Incidentally, written at the bottom of the page with the original writing on was this:-

God bless all who search, for without the searchers no truth can prevail.

I like this quotation, I hope you do too.

Sincerely Alexa.

LET US HELP
****

Your needs are varied with each waking dawn.
Your lifestyle such that calm may not ensue.
As consciousness returns new thoughts are born,
In hazy daze, not knowing what to do.
Now hearken to your guides and hear their call.
They surround you, to guard, direct and love.
Perhaps you stumble, perhaps you headlong fall.
Then hold to spirit, who with whom you move.
We anxiously and continually wait.
We earnestly beg you, to have no fear.
Accrete with us, do not procrastinate
We accede to all you ask, we are here.
Come draw us nigh, let us and love surround you.
Come feel our thoughts and guidance freely given.
Dissenting thoughts shall be no more to hound you.
Down on your knees and thank God in his heaven.

SWIFT
21 May 1979.

ANNOTATION
(Swift's rant)

Phew!! I've had to stop a minute and get my breath back. What a criticism of man. We all know that what he says in this epistle is true, and I for one am completely on his side.
It would seem that even in the next life they can see that man can not get his act together.
One of my favourite home made clichés,(and I often expound it), is "This world is a beautiful place, it is just full of men made of shit."
Do you agree? Don't be shy of e.mailing me.
alexapope@yahoo.es
(Sorry about the bad word.)

Sincerely Alexa

OK

SWIFT'S RANT
****

Deep in the pit of man's despotic mind,
A turmoil rages, torn with eyes of fire.
Is man, so much of hell, he cannot find
His sensitive ideas cull naught but ire.
Develop well this theme, now, Hades child.
Does reason, thought, and love lie cold once more?
Can all the teachers past nie drive them wild?
Or, are all souls destined for hell's own shore?
A split in atoms hurls man to his doom.
A split in minds own realms, annihilates,
The very reasoned waves which may exhume,
The curdling ghost which hauls man to his fates.
My heart no longer beats for man's redemption.
My suffocating soul cries out for air
All are damned, all, all, without exemption.
The Devil waits, serene in his own lair.

SWIFT
22.August 1985.

ANNOTATION
(Prayer of obedience)

Here is a nice prayer to finish off book number five. I do sometimes get a lot of nice blendings, but sometimes Dean Swift has a little rant and rave when something rattles his cage, just as I do, and I'm sure you do too sometimes.
Well here we are at the end of these thirty writings, which means I am half way through the task I have been asked to do. I do hope you have enjoyed these little annotations, now i have to dig out some more original epistles.
May your God go with you,

Love and sincerity as always,

Alexa.

A PRAYER OF OBEDIENCE

****

Oh holy essence of wondrous beauty,
Around my heart your loving tendrils curl.
Elate my soul and will my flesh to duty,
Teach our souls, my God, to still unfurl.
As the spirit in me blossoms and ever grows.
As the service rooted flesh walks ever stronger.
The peace within wells up, God always knows,
Of needs we have, without his strength we hunger.
We soldier on from day to day, well knowing.
The love of God is for our furtherance.
With ever widening psyche, spirits growing.
In purest divinity, receive our utterance.

SWIFT
5th February 1980

End of book five

AND
For buying my book

e. mail. alexapope@yahoo.es

www.ingramcontent.com/pod-product-compliance
Ingram Content Group UK Ltd.
Pitfield, Milton Keynes, MK11 3LW, UK
UKHW021011200726
13857UKWH00004B/1390

9 781847 992543